SEARCH
for
TOMORROW

UTOPIA
...OR BUST!

PRODUCTS FOR THE PERFECT WORLD

BY PHILIP GARNER

PLEXUS, LONDON

Published by Plexus Publishing Limited
30 Craven Street London WC2N 5NT
First printing 1985

Garner, Philip
Utopia – or bust
I. Title
818'.5409 PS3557.A716/

ISBN 0 85965-094-4

On the front cover: Air Swimming

Acknowledgements
Master Photographer: Tim Street-Porter
Other photographs: Raeanne Giovanni (page 11, 48)
Jeff Cohen (page 40)
Construction of evening suit (page 29): Tony Riviera
Conceptual and editorial assistance: Nancy Reese
Special thanks to Richard Amdur, Richard Schatzburg,
Marilyn Schatzburg, Kathryn Greene and Vikki DiDonato
Art Director: Virginia Rubel
On page 1:
'Search For Tomorrow' Artist's conception of giant ship which will one day ply the countless untold miles of space and eons of time in relentless pursuit of the inevitable but elusive alien being.

TO ST. THOMAS MORE

"Thus, trained in all learning, the minds of the Utopians are exceedingly apt in the invention of the arts which promote the advantage and convenience of life."

—St. Thomas More,
from his book UTOPIA,
first published in 1516

TABLE OF CONTENTS

"People in all parts of the world have dreams of UTOPIA."

INTRODUCTION

My friends,

I thank you for the great success of my first book, THE BETTER LIVING CATALOG. Your overwhelming response to such items as the PALMBRELLA, FORKOMB, BLASTER BRA and SHOWER-IN-A-CAN has reassured me that the world has not outgrown its need for LSD (Labor Saving Devices). I feel well rewarded for my efforts. The resulting extension of my personal credit has enabled me to enlarge my research and development (R&D) facilities and to access much-needed technical apparatuses. As you can see, affluence and notoriety have not swayed me from my goals and I am more than ever committed to the conquest and abolition of drudgery as we know it.

It gives me great pleasure to bring you this second volume. It contains my very latest work which, as you may perceive, has taken a slightly more theoretical direction. I will explain why. Not long ago, I observed that the world is practically bursting at the seams with mass-produced contraptions. I

shower-in-a-can

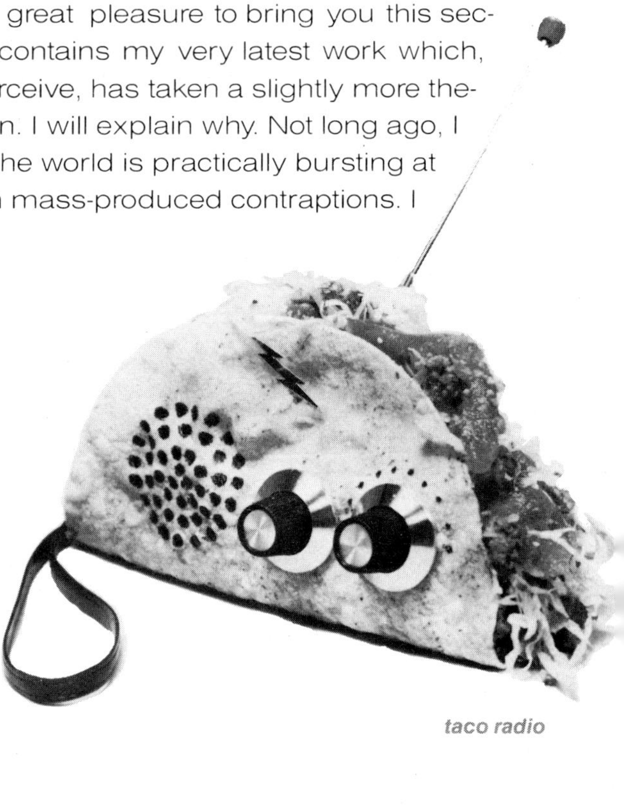

taco radio

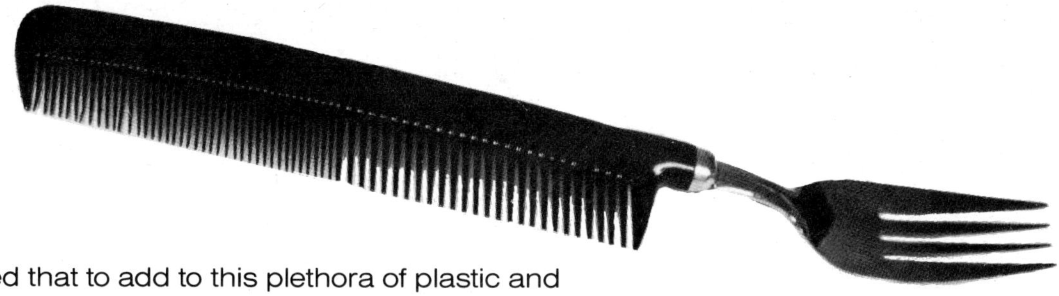

concluded that to add to this plethora of plastic and pot-metal paraphernalia would be to misuse my penchant for pixilated predictions. I resolved to look beyond the limitations of the work-a-day world, to reach for the stars, to attempt to think the impossible thought, to "go for it," as it were. I mustered all my strength, courage, fortitude, initiative and willpower, took a deep breath and set upon the ultimate challenge. I would be undeterred by the failure of countless, untold visionaries throughout the pages of human history. I would seek and find that state of immortal bliss, U T O P I A! In the spirit of our tenacious forefathers, the pioneers, I chose for my motto, "UTOPIA OR BUST!" I invite you then, through the medium of this book, to accompany me on the first leg of this dynamic and inspiring journey. Slip into some sensible shoes and, of course, a thinking cap, and let's go together to the perfect world.

forkomb

Philip Garner

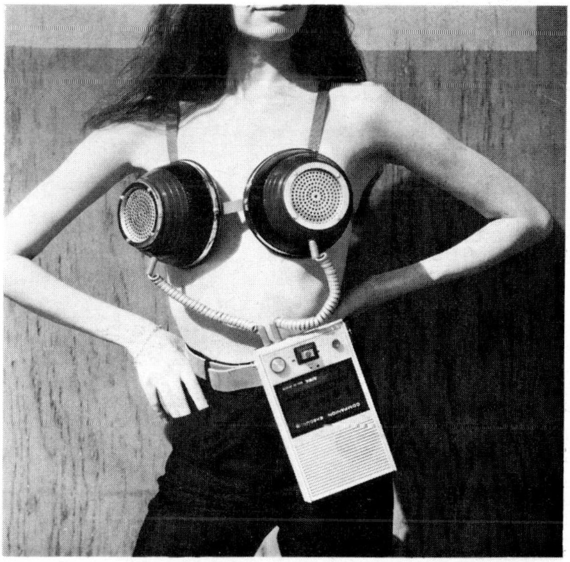

blaster bra

LOST & FOUND HORIZONS

"Tomorrow is the question."

—Ornette Coleman (early album title)

THOUGHTSPACE *(Personal Headquarters)*

Style: Future American

Home "knowledge bank" computer terminal is in image of human head and flanked by coil suspension relax-o-chairs. Organic-style "doubl-loveseat" is covered in peppermint-scented material. Other features include "bust-out" picture window, "stoned" TV and laser "beam" ceiling.

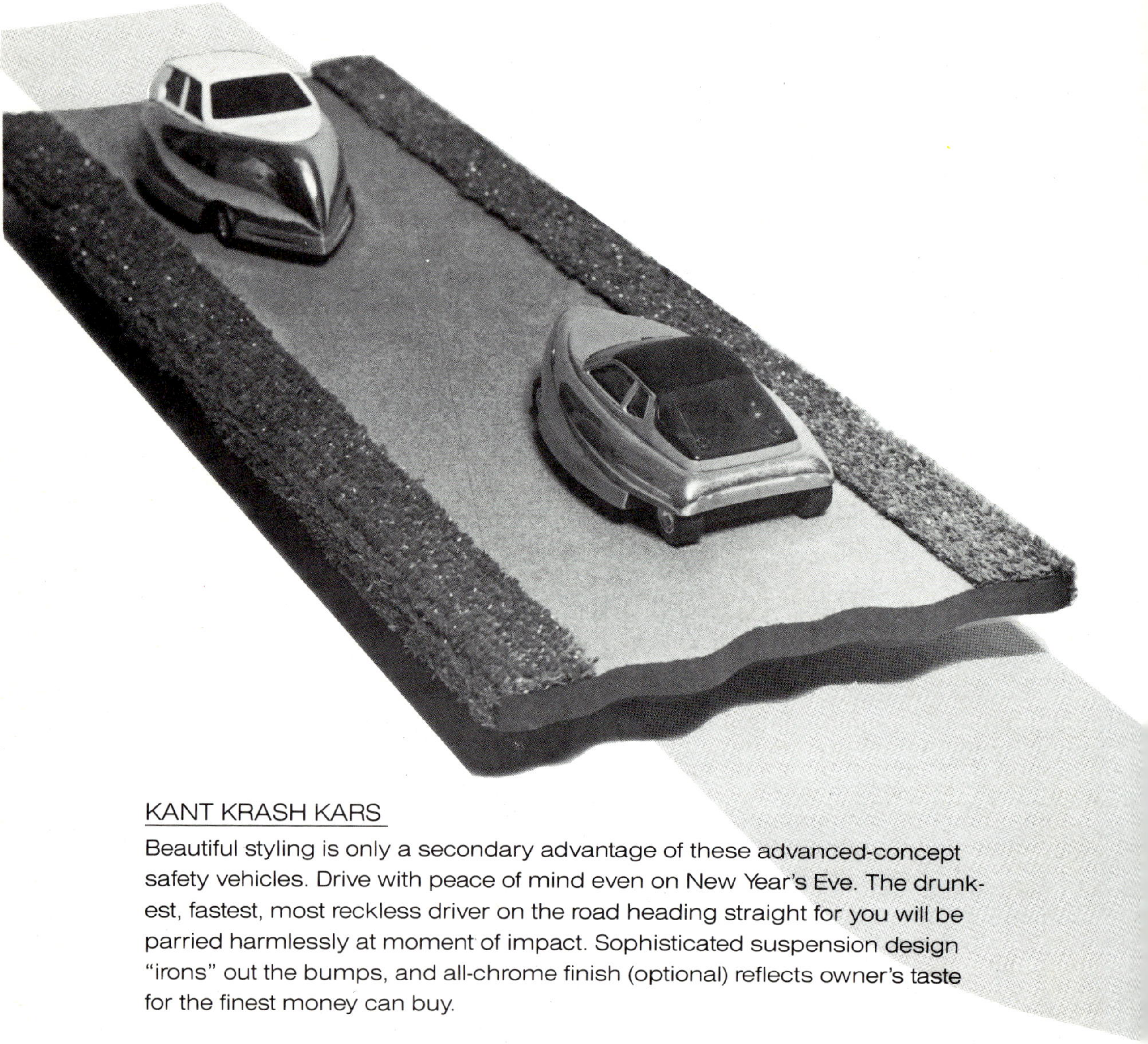

KANT KRASH KARS

Beautiful styling is only a secondary advantage of these advanced-concept safety vehicles. Drive with peace of mind even on New Year's Eve. The drunkest, fastest, most reckless driver on the road heading straight for you will be parried harmlessly at moment of impact. Sophisticated suspension design "irons" out the bumps, and all-chrome finish (optional) reflects owner's taste for the finest money can buy.

PORT-A-PARTY

Fill the social-void by hiring one of the many outcall repertoire companies specializing in "upbeat ambience." The resourceful group shown here has cleverly turned an empty swimming pool into a trendy, subterranean, champagne record hop. Select from "mild to wild" effects depending on your mood and/or the dictates of the occasion.

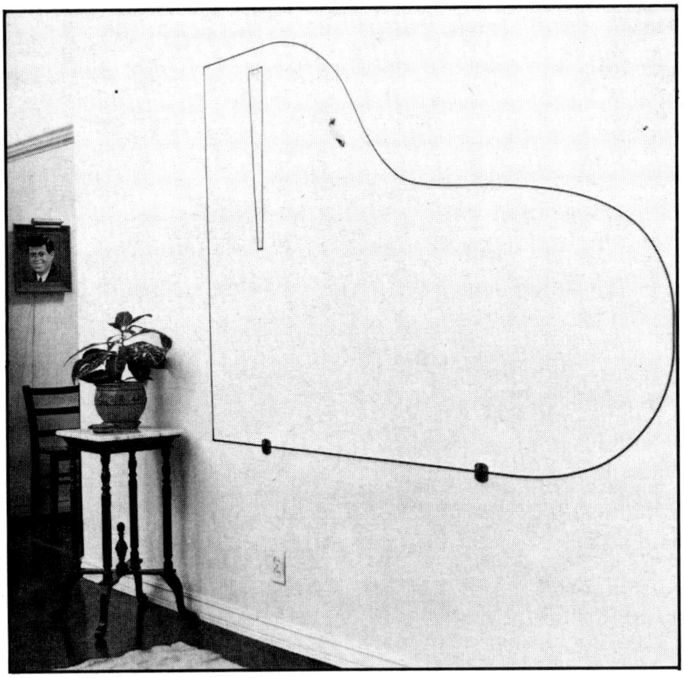

"MURPHY" GRAND

You may practice the piano six hours a day, but that still leaves eighteen hours that this behemoth of an instrument must take up half of the living room. (Judged an inconvenience by "Consumer's Report.") The "Murf," counter-weighted for ease of operation, is up and out of the way as quickly as you can say: "Johann Sebastian Waller."

VAC-TRAC

High-speed rail vehicle uses propulsion system derived from ordinary household vacuum cleaner, a concept inspired by the maxim: "Banality begets brilliance." Powerful turbo-motor displaces air in front of unit while simultaneously exhausting in aft, as vehicle literally "sucks" itself along track. "Mini-ducts" in passenger cabin carry trash and other waste to removable disposal module in rear.

MOTOBROOM

"The drudgery destroyer" sweeps up to six rooms on a single tank of gas. Variable-stroke powerhead allows greater accuracy and versatility over a variety of sweeping situations. Accessories include bell (shown), light and protective windshield. Two-section handle disassembles so unit can be easily stored in violin case.

WATERPICASSO

It is a known fact that great art is more comprehensible when integrated with the rituals of daily life. Conversely, mundane tasks become enlightened experiences with a dash of that euphoric spice, "profound artistic endeavor." WATERPICASSO exemplifies this notion with a unique highlight: the anguish of the Guernica (front illustration) has an obvious oral emphasis, appropriate for a dental appliance.

BIG BROTHER II

Philco "Holovision" receiver projects life-like image of head of inventor, Garner, for stunning realism at lectures and other engagements which the man himself is unable or unwilling to attend. A number of these devices are available and may be reserved by non-profit organizations and select private parties. Programming covers every subject.

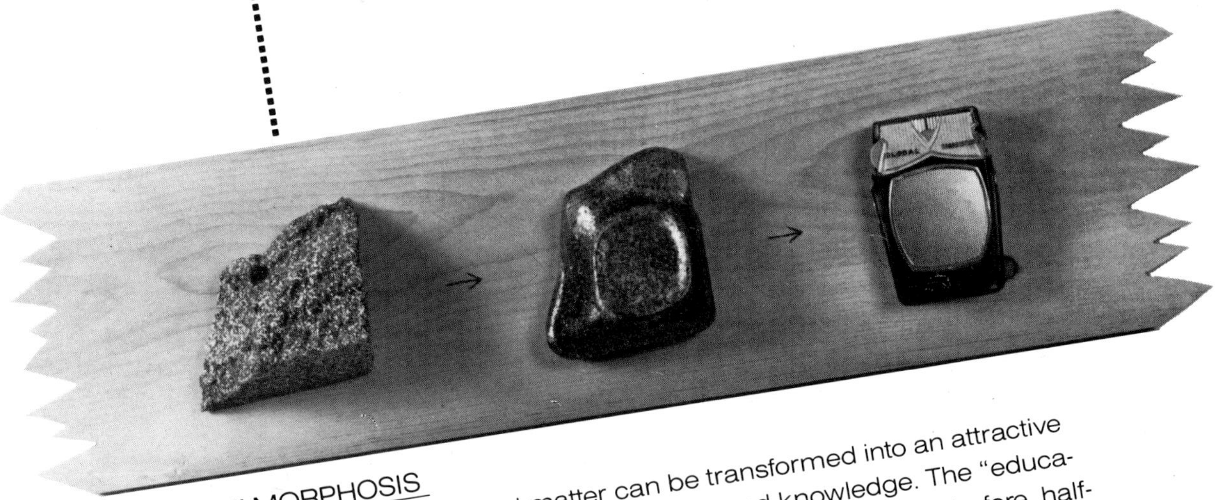

METAMORPHOSIS

Crude, inert, useless natural matter can be transformed into an attractive consumer appliance, thanks to recently gleaned knowledge. The "educational" model shown here illustrates the process in three steps: before, halfway point and after. A technical discussion will be omitted as it would be incomprehensible to the layman.

TWO-IN-ONE APPLIANCE

An example of the "new wave" in home appliances, this double-duty device interfaces two types of energy, heat and light, with subtle simultaneity. Monofunction units, still in widespread use, are inefficient, unsightly and a threat to the ecological balance.

HEAD HOLSTERS

Cerebral security system. Just a "dummy" but reminds plagiarists, parasites, rip-off artists and deadbeats to do their <u>own</u> thinking for a change. As a bonus, the product also protects against theft of garments and precious stones/metals worn about the head.

OBJECT ON VIEW

This one-creature "mini-zoo" marks the return to vogue of a great American travel treat, the "roadside attraction." Now that appropriate legislation has been passed, many such diversionary installations will be springing up along the nation's superhighways. The "Mouse Park" (shown) is also a tribute to modern biology. This oversize but affectionate fellow was bred especially for roadside amusement duty.

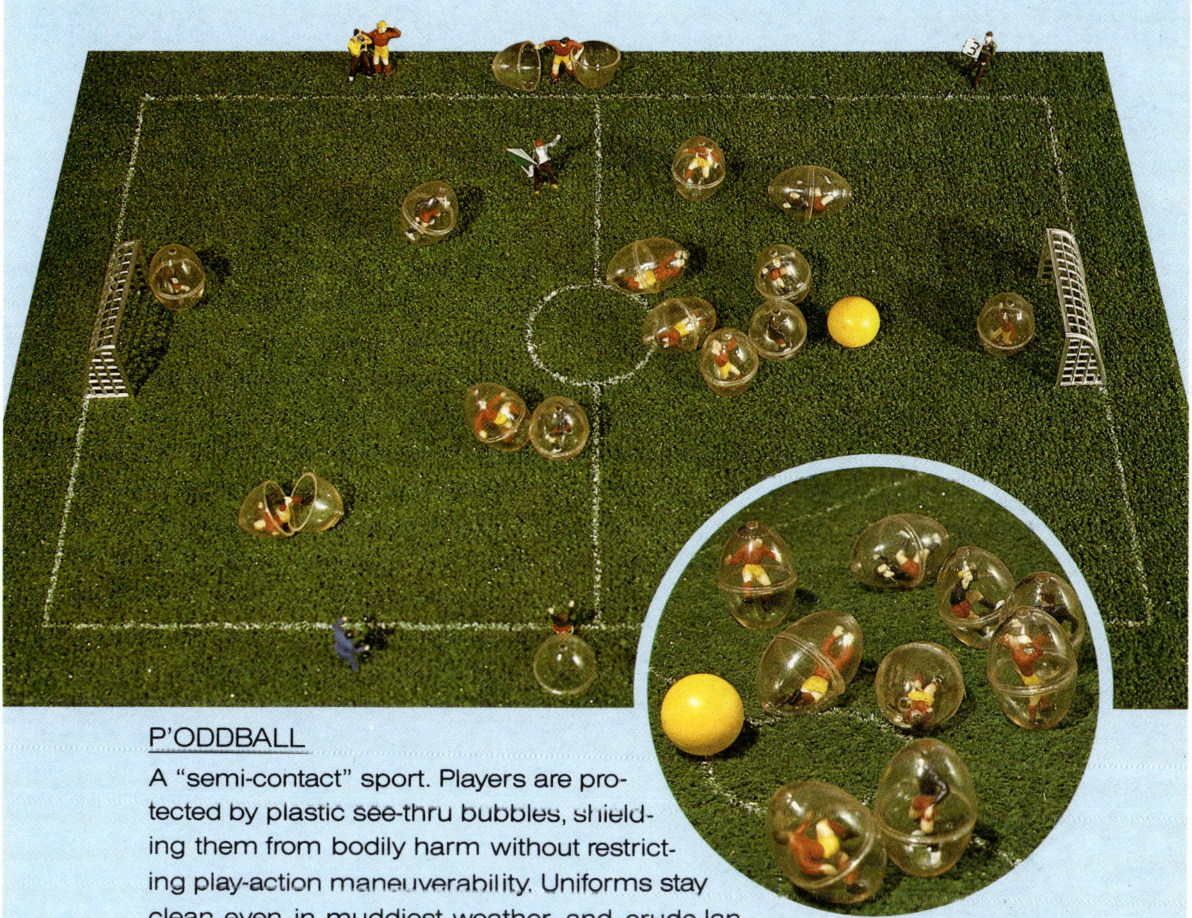

P'ODDBALL

A "semi-contact" sport. Players are protected by plastic see-thru bubbles, shielding them from bodily harm without restricting play-action maneuverability. Uniforms stay clean even in muddiest weather, and crude language, not uncommon in sporting events, is inaudible to the crowd. As a bonus, equipment may be carried to and from the playing field in the pods.

OUTBOARD MOTORCYCLE

"Nauti-Bike" is a marriage of land and sea vehicular components. Unit features front and rear steering for unprecedented maneuverability and can be quickly disassembled for transporting. Any standard outboard motor from 1 1/2 to 200 horsepower can be used (3 1/2 HP shown).

A TOUCH O' CLASS

State-subsidized luxury automobile rides permit those of straitened circumstances to experience the opulence of the elite for the price of a wad of bubblegum, thus alleviating social unrest. Furthermore, manufacturers are encouraged to produce more and still finer examples of this acclaimed domestic commodity, the "dreamboat" class motor car.

TOMORROW IN REVIEW

"Never leave well enough alone."

—Raymond Loewy

HAUTE S'COUTURE

Recycled road unit adds a kinetic note to the well-appointed but static interior. Prestigious Italian styling is highlighted by functional features such as sound system (replacing power unit), underseat storage for magazines, cigars, etc., mood lighting and accent fringe.

TROYOTA *(The Trojan Car)*

Giant wooden automobile is party-crash tested and holds up to fifty uninvited guests. Car is presented anonymously to host and hostess, thereby penetrating the social barrier. When "gift" is safely on the premises, "passengers" devehicle (get out) and discreetly mix with invitees.

SINNET

Thought by some to be the world's most challenging game, few players have ever had the skill or patience to master its subtle techniques. In fact, the fanaticism and unswerving devotion demanded of those who take up SINNET have limited its appeal to obscure cults in little-known places. Mass popularity will have to wait until the evolutionary process has endowed the human animal with a new level of hypercoordination. Note to beginners: learn "tennis" first, a much easier game.

ALLIGATOR SOUP

A leathery swamp-broth served by the crock, à la Reptiliano. May be reconstituted from worn or out-of-style handbags, shoes and belts. (An acquired taste.)

VIEILLE CUISINE

The dish that prompted the switch in popularity to Nouvelle Cuisine. "Boeuf Gros" comprises an entire roast ox pneumatically compressed into a "patty" the size of a meat loaf. It is not surprising that the TV tray in the photograph was not up to the task of supporting such an anomaly.

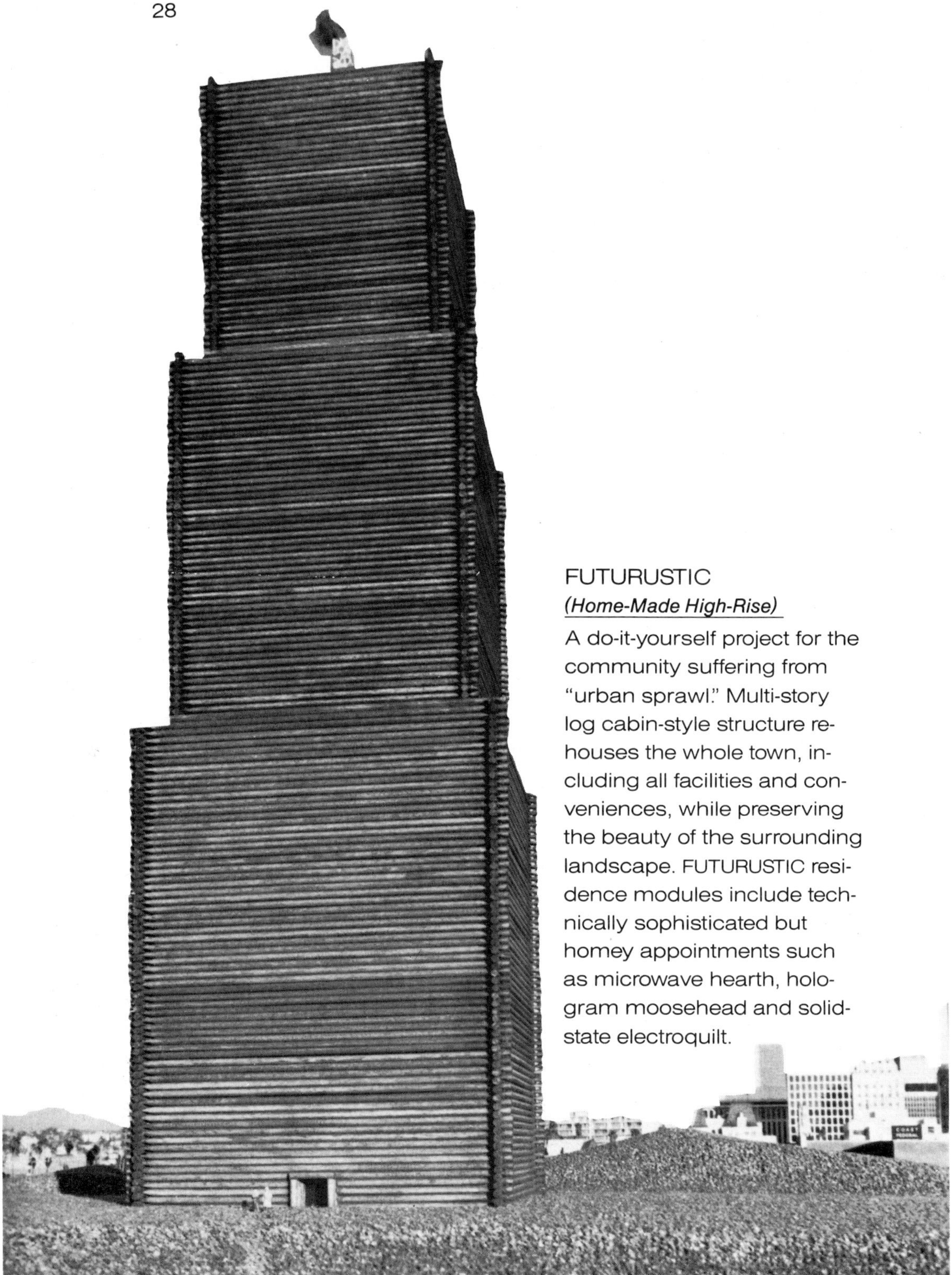

FUTURUSTIC
(Home-Made High-Rise)

A do-it-yourself project for the community suffering from "urban sprawl." Multi-story log cabin-style structure re-houses the whole town, including all facilities and conveniences, while preserving the beauty of the surrounding landscape. FUTURUSTIC residence modules include technically sophisticated but homey appointments such as microwave hearth, hologram moosehead and solid-state electroquilt.

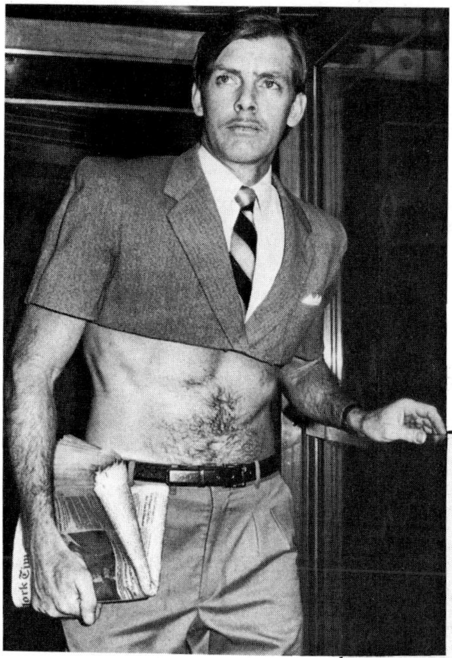

EVENING SUIT

Sequel to the ever popular "half-suit" (left), this garment reflects the "new honesty" in male-female role referencing. Bare shoulders express "male vulnerability" as well as permitting the use of "body English," a communication mode proven effective for conferences, speeches and intimate encounters.

1

OBSERVATION PIT / INSPECTACLES

(1) Fully equipped "scrutinizing facility" allows the user to make casual or deeply perceptive observations with maximum efficiency. Attention may be directed toward an object, another person or merely a concept, thanks to "universal" inner-chamber design. (2) INSPECTACLES have "input amplification" capability and, when used within O.P., the keenness with which one may perceive relevant data on the object of concentration is unparalleled. OBSERVATION PIT is located in Sensory City, California.

TRANSISTOR TERROR

Our current fascination with miniaturization may backfire if we don't act now! Squeezing transistors, chips and other components down to miniscule proportions and cramming them into claustrophobic cases is probably causing tension and pressure within these modules which will one day reach the bursting point, posing an insidious threat to the millions who own or use these devices. Be a good citizen. Let your miniaturized appliance out of its case now and thwart the threat.

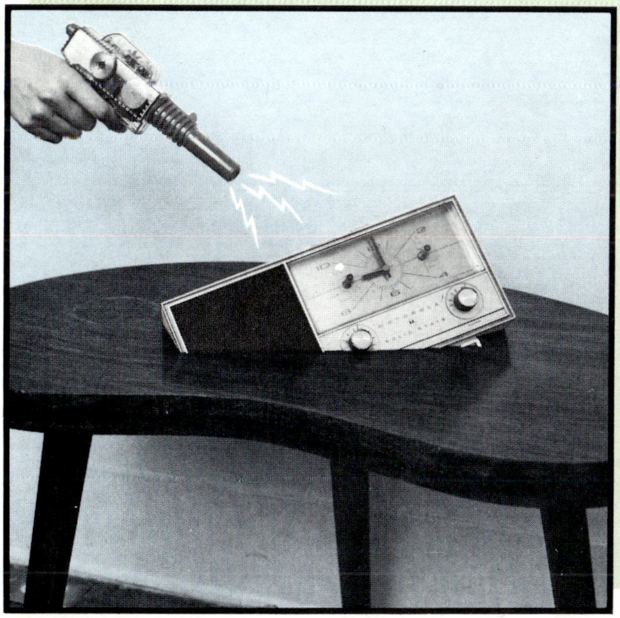

FUTUREGAG

Hi-tech pranksters can now sink appliances by "molecular interactive" principle. Gun is harmless to people and pets but try to get that clock-radio back up out of the table! It can't be done. A great gag at parties, business meetings and other social occasions.

Express

Local

LONG-DISTANCE MOVING SIDEWALKS

Clearly the simplest, most unobtrusive, efficient and versatile mass-transit system known to man, MOVING SIDEWALKS were a "closet concept" when relegated only to airport terminals. Moderate-speed interurban "MSW" system features "infinistop," which permits mounting or dismounting at any point along route. Superfast cross-country system connects major cities, and riders can sleep on walkway for overnight trips. Remember: "A sidewalk that doesn't move isn't worth its weight in cement."

Before

BUSSTER

World's largest two-passenger sports car! Everyone dreams of being "King (or Queen) of the Road" at one time or another, and now the hardware exists to make that dream a reality. Vehicle features rear-mounted diesel engine with automatic transmission. Vast under-hood storage area accommodates outboard runabout, folding sports-plane and a massive quantity of recreational and personal paraphernalia.

THOUGHT REMOVER

An electric "blank-it" which obliterates recurring nightmares, bothersome memories, pesky statistics and tedious trivia. The brain's memory bank is a container and, as such, has a maximum capacity. Shoveling out obsolete information like old song titles, auto engine specifications and names of distant relatives makes way for lucid reception of up-to-the-minute input and clear, precise thinking.

Dress

Sport

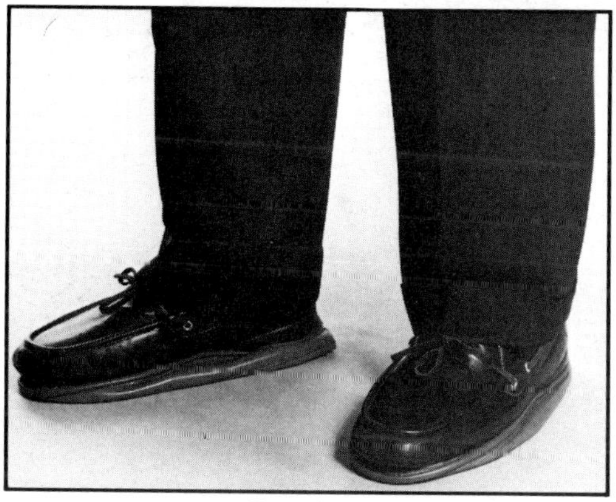

Business

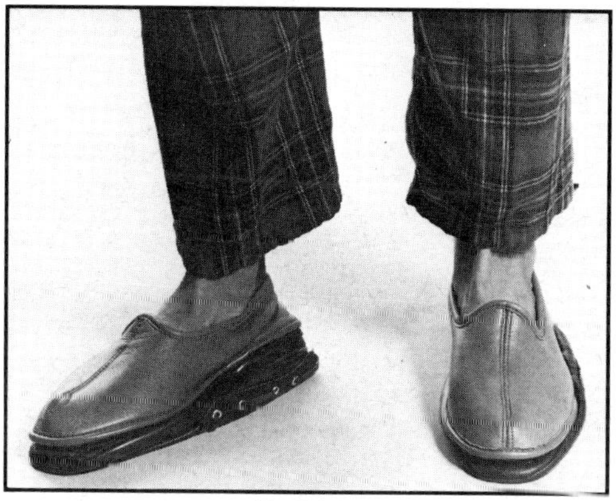

Bedtime

REVERSAPPAREL

"Quickchange" may be the byword of the 21st century. As the "technomadic" lifestyle (currently enjoyed by the retired camper/pickup set) becomes a universal necessity, personal "space" will be sharply curtailed. Multifunctional personal accessories such as the REVERSAPPAREL shown here are space-efficient and allow the wearer to "transition" between contrasting activities at a moment's notice.

SOMEONE FOR EVERYTHING

"If he is an artist, as well as a designer, he will accomplish this in a way that will arouse an unusual amount of interest in the onlooker."

—Norman Bel Geddes

"FLORI-CAL" SUNSHINE INTERLINK

Tropical tunnelway provides direct connection between the two most popular American resort states, Florida and California. Travel efficiently, securely and free from distracting geography, time-robbing roadside attractions and health-imperiling climatic changes. Unbroken 3,000 mile tube features all necessary conveniences, built-in and coin-operated.

STATUE OF PUBERTY *(artist's conception)*

A proposed monument to be constructed in the harbor of Los Angeles, California. Giant velvet-covered female bust looms majestically from the placid Pacific. All facial features contain lookout points, while back of head is world's largest satellite communications dish. Navel provides underwater observation port and the breasts house emergency foodstuffs (left) and cultural time capsule (right).

ALIENATURE

Discovered recently in one of our national forests, this broken branch, packed to the bark with technology, suggests some horseplay on the part of aliens, foreigners or both: Does this specimen indicate that the entire "forest" was an ingenious mechanical facsimile, or was it merely a plant? The question remains unanswered, as the photographer became frightened and left quickly when he sensed that the trees were staring woodenly at him. A "sticky" situation.

BACKWARDS CAR

Representing the Post-Neo-Renaissance tolerance for personal expression, BACKWARDS CARS are literally "vehicles" of opposition to the "oldthink" credo of conformity. A popular model for this conversion, the 1959 Chevrolet Biscayne, 2-door (shown) is also a monument to the bygone era of corporate artistic expression.

INDUSTRIAL PARK

This intellectual and technological playground is, in fact, a nomadic nerve-center run by gypsy geniuses and transient technicians. Attractive woodgrain "modulabs" are actually hovering land barges. Entire complex can be relocated in hours.

GLASS-BOTTOM BUS

Designed in response to those perceptive and discerning tourists who demand more than just pretty scenery from their bus tours. Close scrutiny of the road surface provides a wealth of cultural information about the inhabitants and general character of the area being visited. These snapshots, taken by a foreign glass-bottom bus tourist, are a case in point. Note the intensity and breadth of insight which they impart.

PILLOW HAT

"Drop out" at a moment's notice for a revitalizing nap. Return to work or recreational activity free from "heavy-lid syndrome" and restored to peak efficiency. Frequent use molds hair into popular "block" style. Overstuff for comfort, quiet and head protection against falling objects.

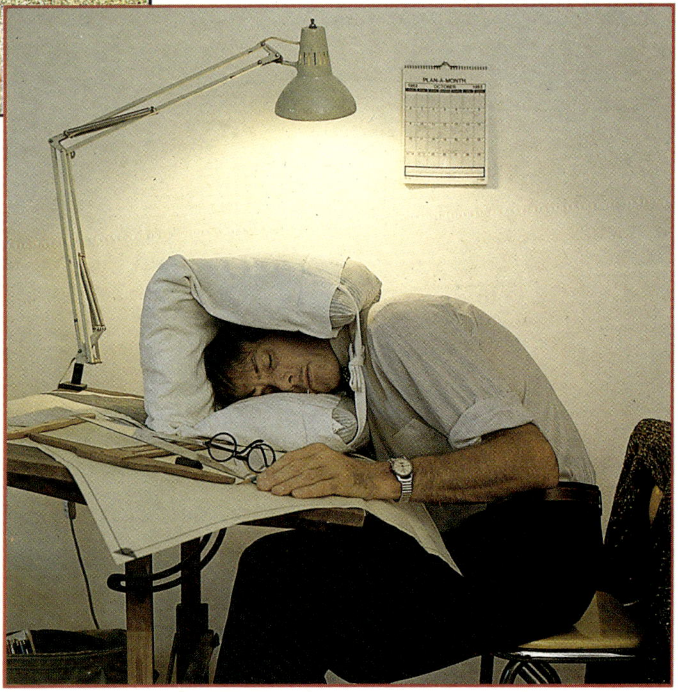

Aerohelmet ***Aerohelmet II*** ***"Hairodynamics"***

HELMET RACING

An aesthetic interface of physical performance and technological innovation, HELMET RACING introduces a new breed, the Techno-athlete. Air turbulence at the roar of the head will no longer prevent the superbly trained bodies of today's super-sportspersons from achieving maximum speed. Participants must excel in aeronautical engineering as well as possessing the usual bodily attributes, adding an intellectual note to the sport.

AIR HOCKEY II

An exciting techno-sport which pits man and machine against man and machine. High-powered backpack blowers are used to blast ball into opponent's goal. Skilled pit crew is as important as "man on the field."

inside

ENERGYM

Top athletes must train relentlessly, lifting tons of weight, running countless miles and in many other ways expending huge amounts of energy. It is almost shocking, with today's need for conservation, that this great source of "natural power" should go untapped. ENERGYM is the answer. Sportspersons operate pumps, generators and other energy-producing machinery as they train, thus making a valuable contribution to a power-hungry world, while simultaneously honing their muscles to contest-level perfection. Inspired by the proud interface of sportsmanship and citizenship, athletes would train as never before.

PERMAFASHION SPORTS JACKET

It's a lifetime investment. Purchased during childhood, the jacket is initially a one-piece outfit. As owner grows up, pants may be worn for comfort and respectability. Graffiti and other personal additions over the years make the garment a treasured and functional "scrapbook."

"Zig-Zag" *"Super-Brow"*

"Umpteen in One"

UNGLASSES

Character accents for those suffering from blandness of feature. A complete "identity system" when you own several pairs of the "umpteen in one" infinitely adjustable model (inset). A breakthrough in Poptometry.

E-Z LIVING ROOM

Style: Space Colonial

Super-plush "thousand leg" chairs allow ultimate enjoyment of "audio tower," a sci-fi/hi-fi module housing sound equipment, planter and gooseneck lamps. Sunken fireplace, "solar grotto" and bus windows complete the effect of this space-age personal nook.

THE BIRTH OF TIME

Proof-positive that everything starts somewhere, even that cagey, master of deceit, TIME itself. The phenomenon of "clock-breeding," a passion of the fastidiously punctual, has also provided valuable research data verifying the existence of perpetual motion, spontaneous combustion and infinity.

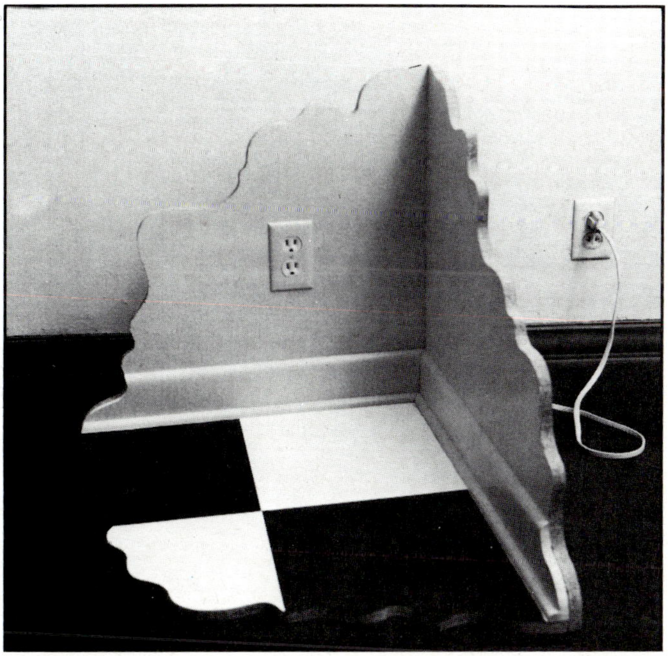

"LE OUTLET"

Built-in, Euro-style ambience elevates this extension cord from the mundane to the magnificent. When remote electrical power is needed, and the occasion demands the extraordinary, select this lovely home accessory. Motifs range from Renaissance (shown) to rustic.

THEME LIVING

"We have to keep our minds open and our mouths shut until we know something."
—from the film "Tarantula"

GRAZING ROBOT *(artist's conception)*

As machines take over more and more of the tasks of man we must anticipate as best we can the eventualities of this usurpation. An "unnatural history" museum of the not-too-distant future might display a diorama such as this one. Will the "Roboticow" also provide us with delicious milk and tender, juicy steaks or will "he" merely exploit our dwindling natural resources? Moral: Perceive and prevent the perils of perverted programming.

BABY "UNITS"

Prototype modular energy sources, shown here in infant stage, represent a very advanced period in the industrial age. Note highly individualized appearance of units as line of distinction between man and machine becomes more diffused. "Names" of devices suggest interface with human society. No technical information available at this time.

CORDLESS ROTOGLOBE

Two horsepower, four-stroke, air-cooled, single cylinder gas engine spins this fast moving world-facsimile at up to 3600 RPM. Integral automatic clutch system allows engine to be warmed up with orb at rest, also prevents "over-revving" at full throttle. Indoor use requires window-mount extension exhaust pipe. Educational, fun and uses no electricity.

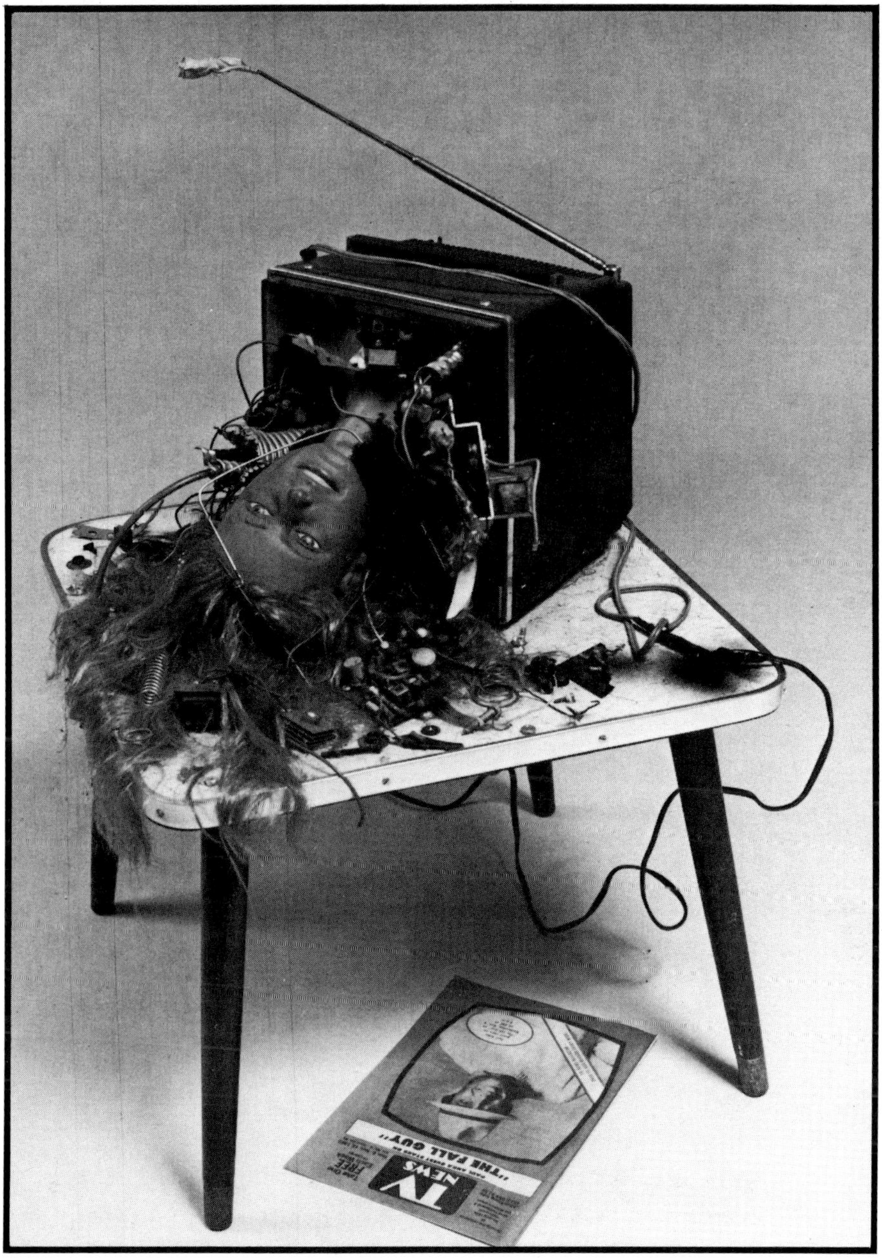

3-D TV

Premature experiments in three-dimensional image transmission can be dangerous, as exemplified by this layman's attempt to convert a conventional set to 3-D during a rerun of the popular "Charlie's Angels" show. Star Farrah has been compromised to say the least! Projects such as this should only be attempted in properly monitored professional research facilities.

BIG BULB

A disturbing speculation on the dangers of runaway energy. Overgrown electric bulbs might literally "burst their fixtures," causing household havoc. How many bulbs do you have in service in your home or place of business? Think about it!

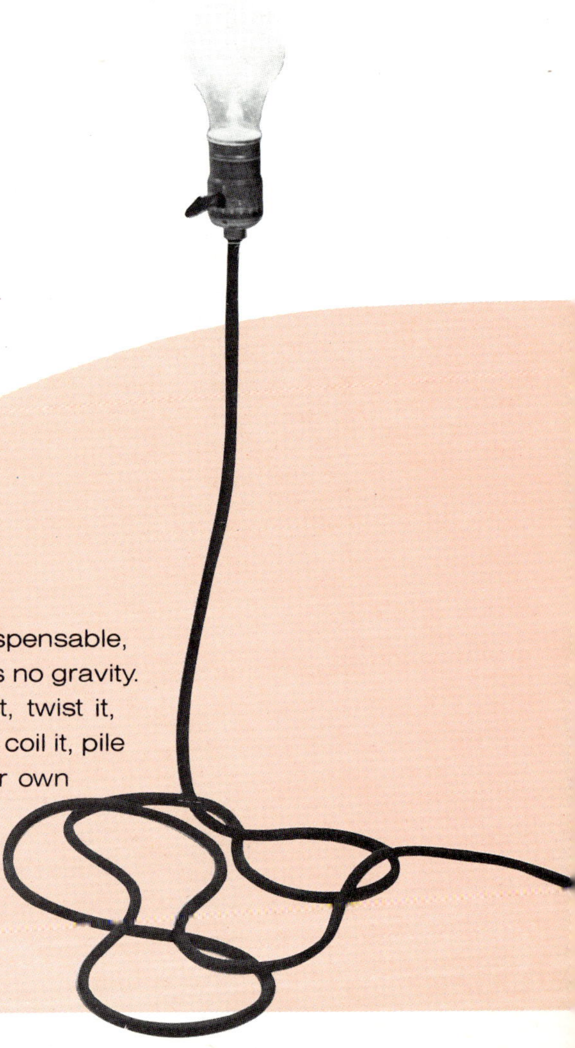

MAGICORD

Simple but indispensable, this cord knows no gravity. Stretch it, knot it, twist it, wrap it, hang it, coil it, pile it or devise your own configurations. Made in India.

HEAD-HUTS

It is now possible for occupants of the same bed to maintain entirely different sleeping schedules and/or nocturnal habits. This multifunctional contrivance muffles snoring and sleep-talking while insulating wearer from activities of bedfellow. Pegboard roof creates effect of starry night when device is used in an illuminated location.

AIR SWIMMING

Self-sealing vinyl "inflate-o-blouses" are filled with light gas to achieve body weight zero. "Human bumper" effect assures personal safety when "swimming" in crowded airspace. Competitive applications range from individual and team racing to "airpolo," in which the ball is inflated to slightly less than zero weight and the players must struggle to keep it aloft.

TEAM JOGGING

In this ultimate test of coordination, a trio of athletes must literally perform as one. "Longsole" shoes provide unexcelled traction for cross-country racing, regardless of terrain or climatic conditions. For supreme endurance tests, center man can actually nap during less strenuous segments of the race and be ready to provide that extra burst of power when the going gets tough. Five-man shoes (not shown) are under development.

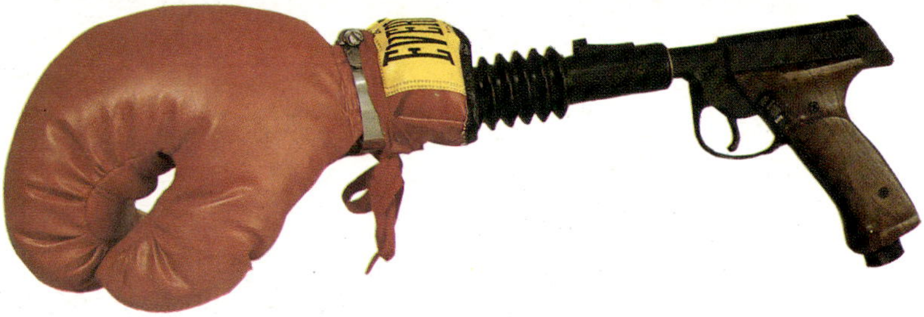

BOXING GUNS

One of man's oldest sports is redefined by "semi-mechanization." Boxers must be fine close-range marksmen, adding an element of chivalry to this traditionally brutal competition. The need to maintain proper range eliminates tedious "clinching."

SKEET BOWLING

A popular indoor sport makes its debut in the great outdoors. Bowling has never reached high status among competitive sports for two reasons: (1) cumbersome equipment, and (2) acrid alley aroma. Skeet shooting is unpopular due to its inaccessibility. SKEET BOWLING juxtaposes the two for a new sporting dynamic. Easily seen "strike" makes this an excellent spectator sport. (Patented launcher maintains airborne pin formation.)

See: 100%   Hear: 0%

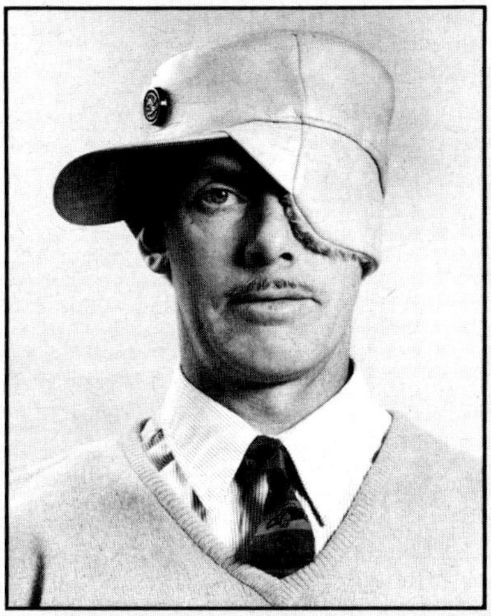

See: 50%   Hear: 50%

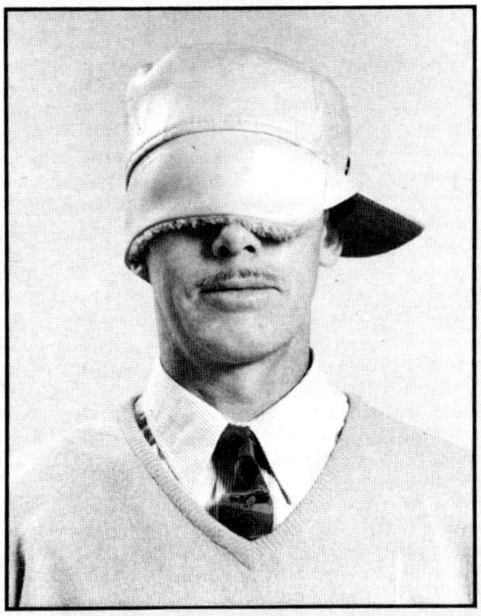

See: 0%   Hear: 50%

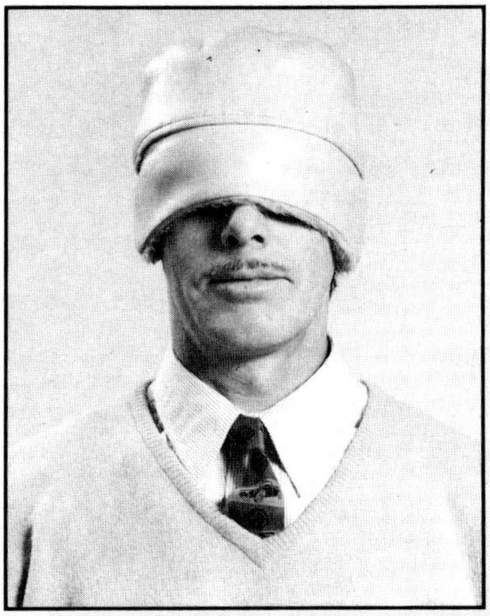

See: 0%   Hear: 0%

ROTARY CONSCIOUSNESS VALVE

Personal and/or social well-being is a direct product of the "reality/fantasy interface." A happy, successful and normally adjusted individual is able to nimbly regulate these influences and maintain a harmonious state of mind. If you lack effective self-control in this area, the "RCV" may be the answer. By placing the unit on your head and revolving it sequentially you can, by progression, inhibit your sensory input, thus controlling internal/external (i.e. fantasy/reality) stimuli.

PERSONAL "BUDDY" MOON

For the individualist who craves companionship without the usual dependency, obligation and consequences thereof. "Dual-mode" switch allows selection of either "stationary hover" or "head orbit." Certified by renowned astronomers as a bona fide celestial body.

WORK IN PROGRESS

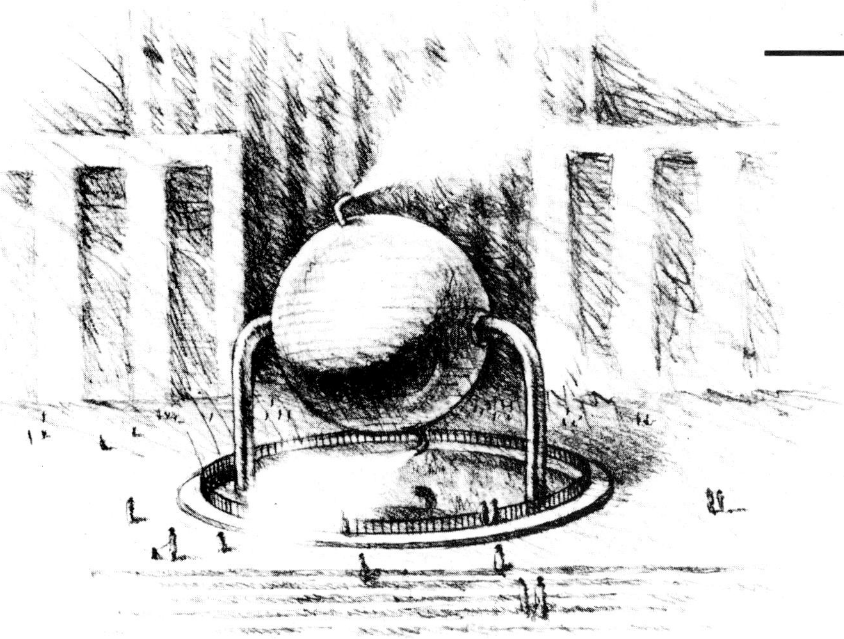

HERO'S ENGINE

steam fountain

RADIO CITY II

MIST-COLLAR

identity obscuring device

PORTRAIT CHAIR

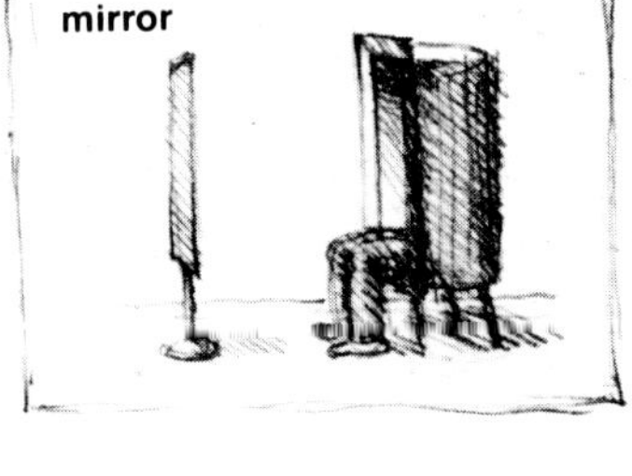

DENETTE

personal male nook

MAGIC MOSS

formerly known as "astroturf"

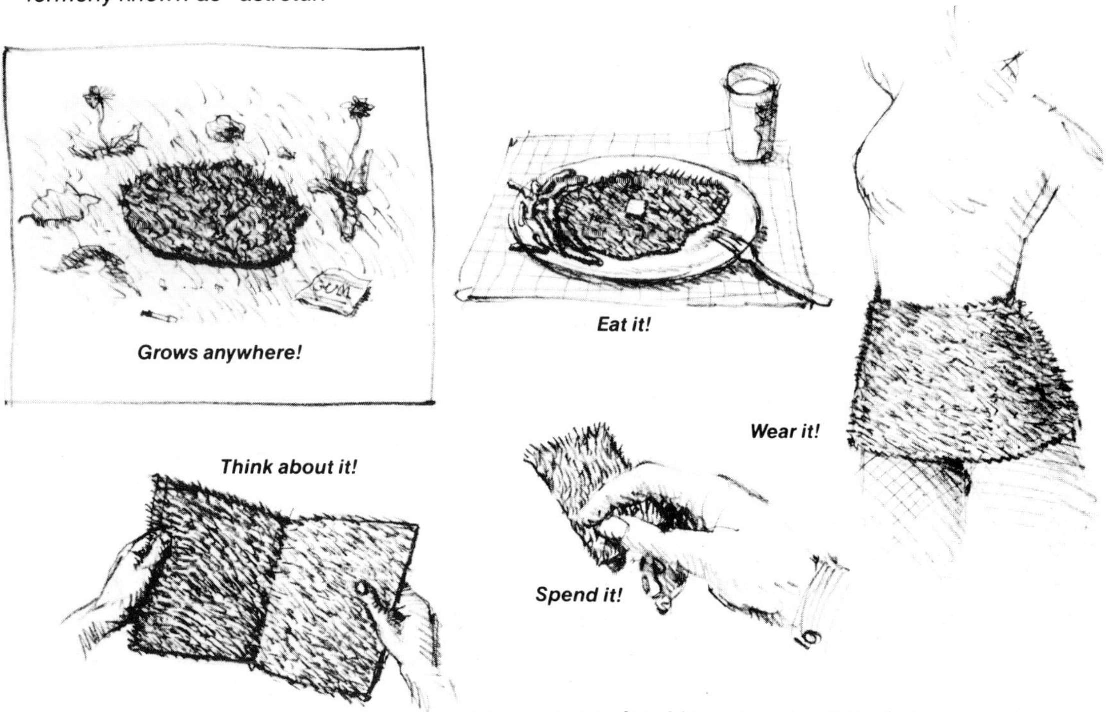

It's warm, comfortable, tasty, attractive, pleasant smelling, easy to maintain, multi-climatic, inexpensive, always appropriate, strong.

KWIK-TOWN

prefab styrofoam community

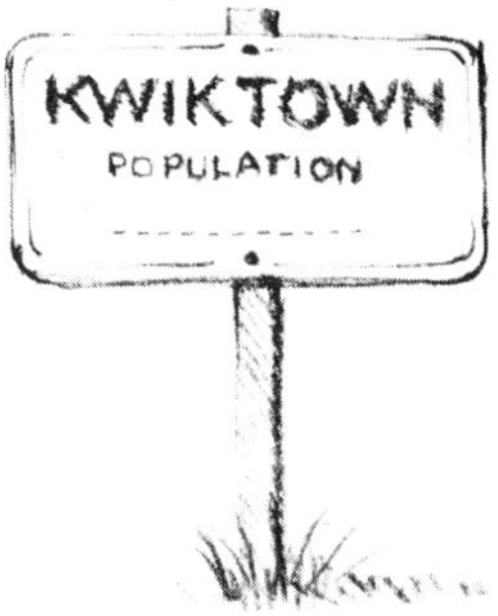

SLOTEL

—5 mph rail cabins
—integrates travel & lodging

HOME PRODUCT MODERNIZER

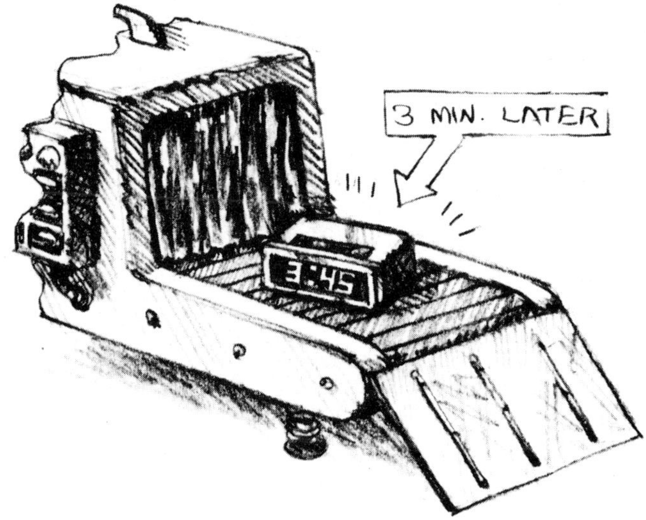

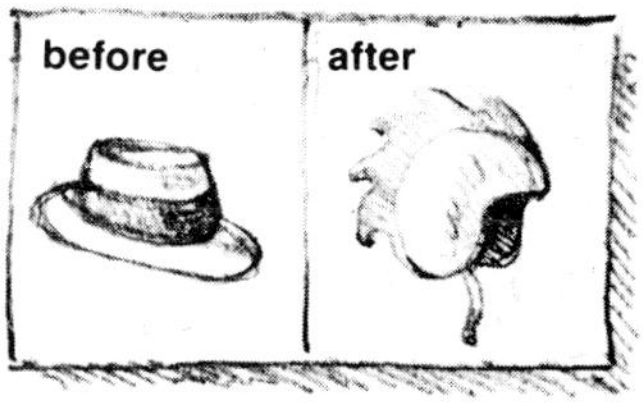

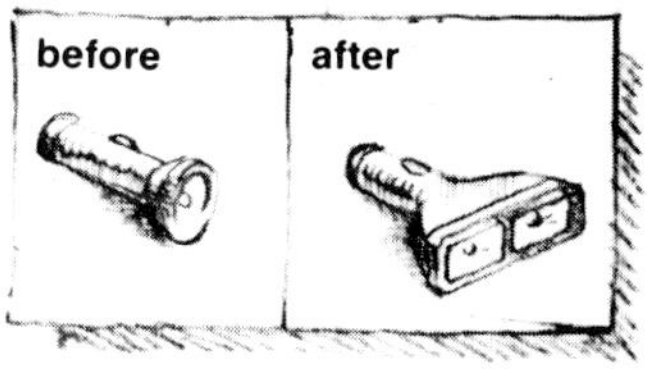

PUBLIC THINK TANK

coin operated

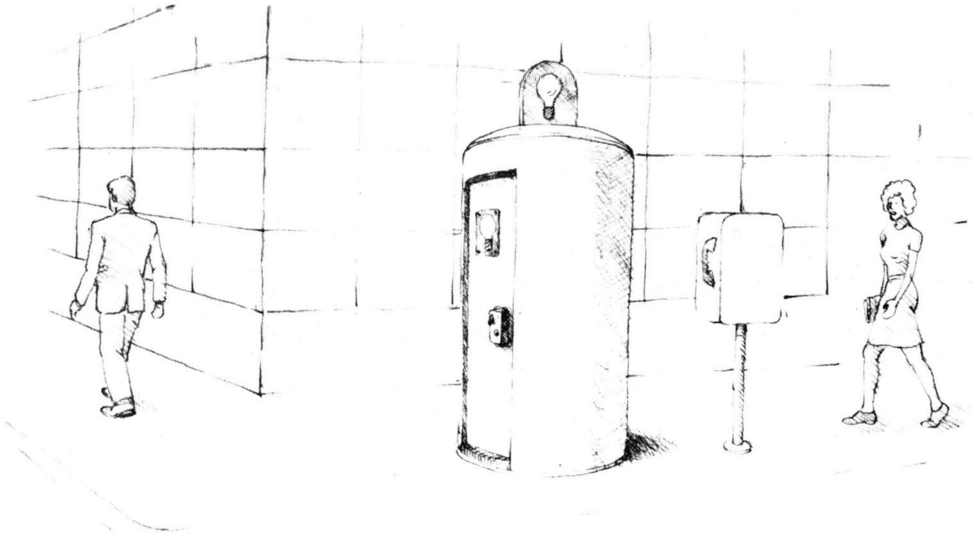

MY DREAM CAR

Phil Garner 1981

'71 Buick Riviera w/ flying bridge

REAL TV DINNER

new "thin" technology

disposable "set" built into lid

UNICULTURE

chopstick conversions

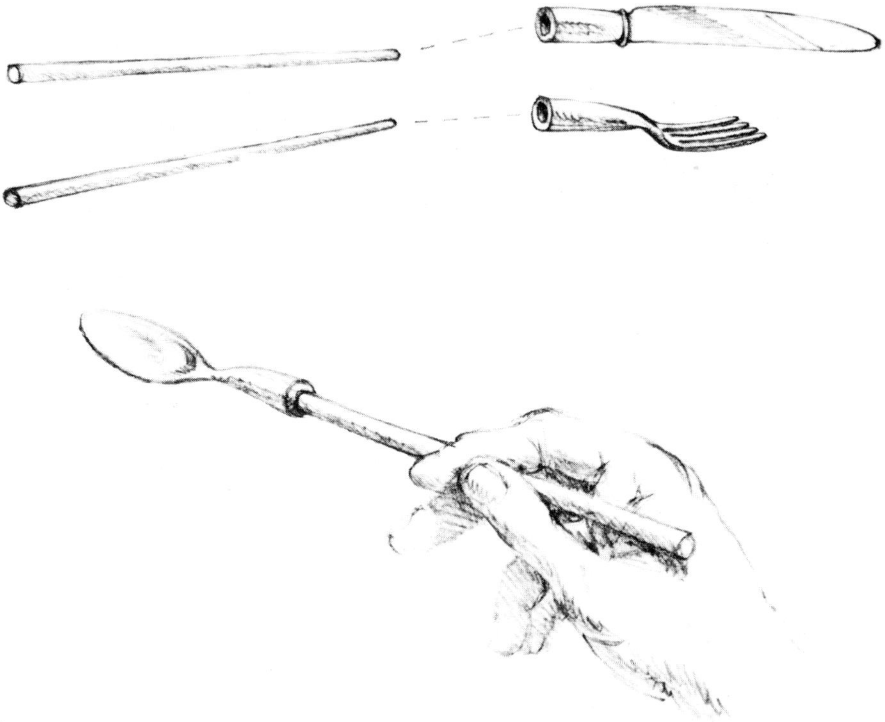

LIMO-RICK

limousine/rickshaw

for:
sporty execs
hi-speed sightseeing

AEROCAR

Semi-blimp

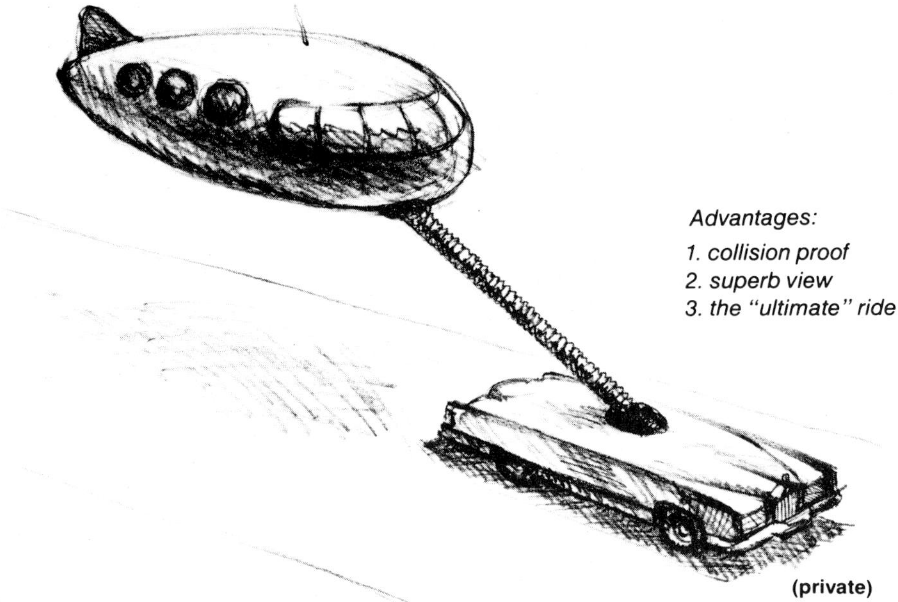

Advantages:

1. *collision proof*
2. *superb view*
3. *the "ultimate" ride*

(private)

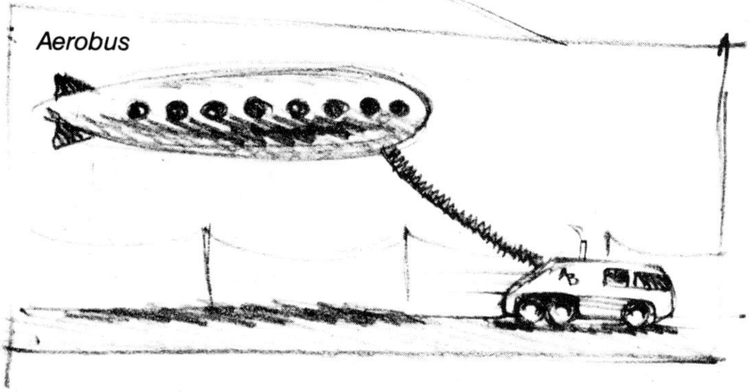

(mass transit)

SUCKER SUB

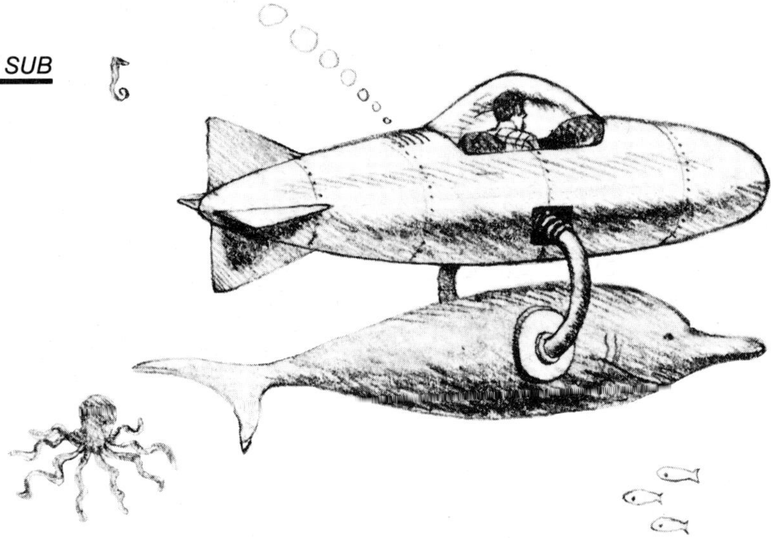

HARNESSING NATURE

plug-in carrot

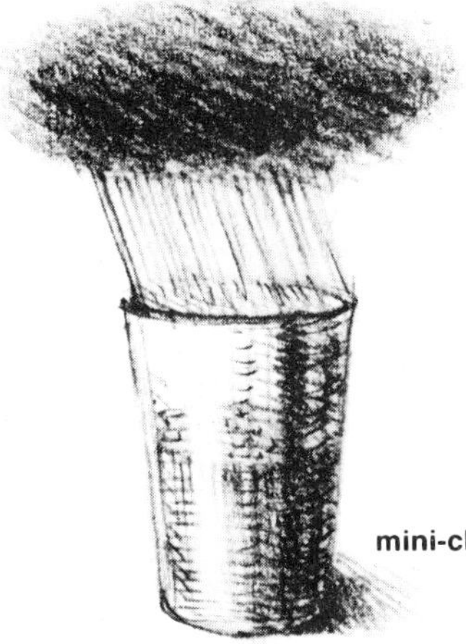

mini-cloud

sweeping willow

"EARTHLING"

secret underground room

entrance

LAZ-R-BOY

contact-disintegrator toilet

ZOO—KINI

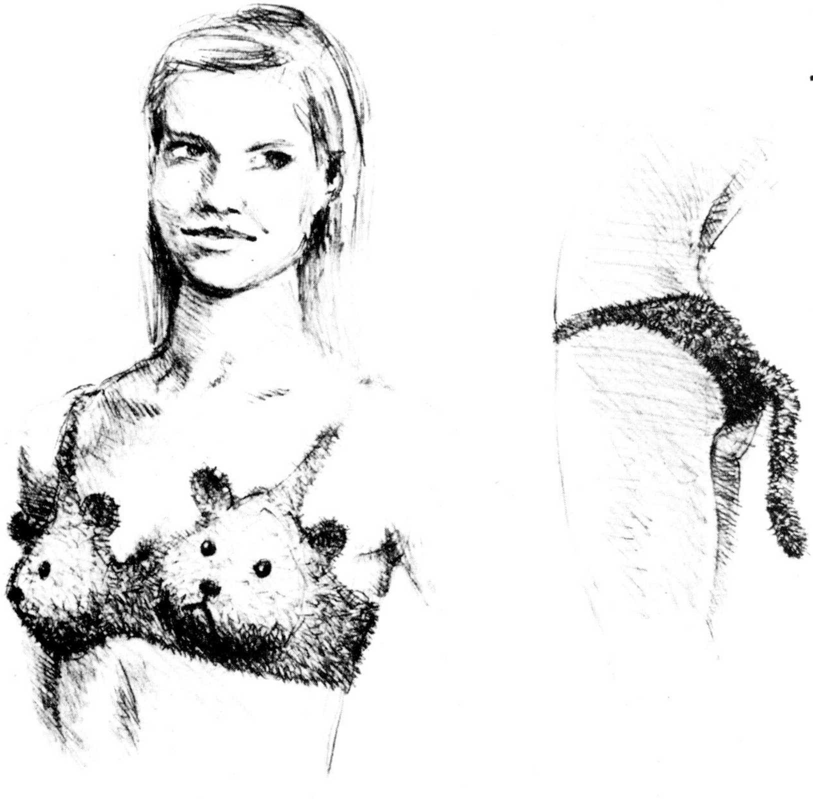

TREE STYLING

PORTAFIRE

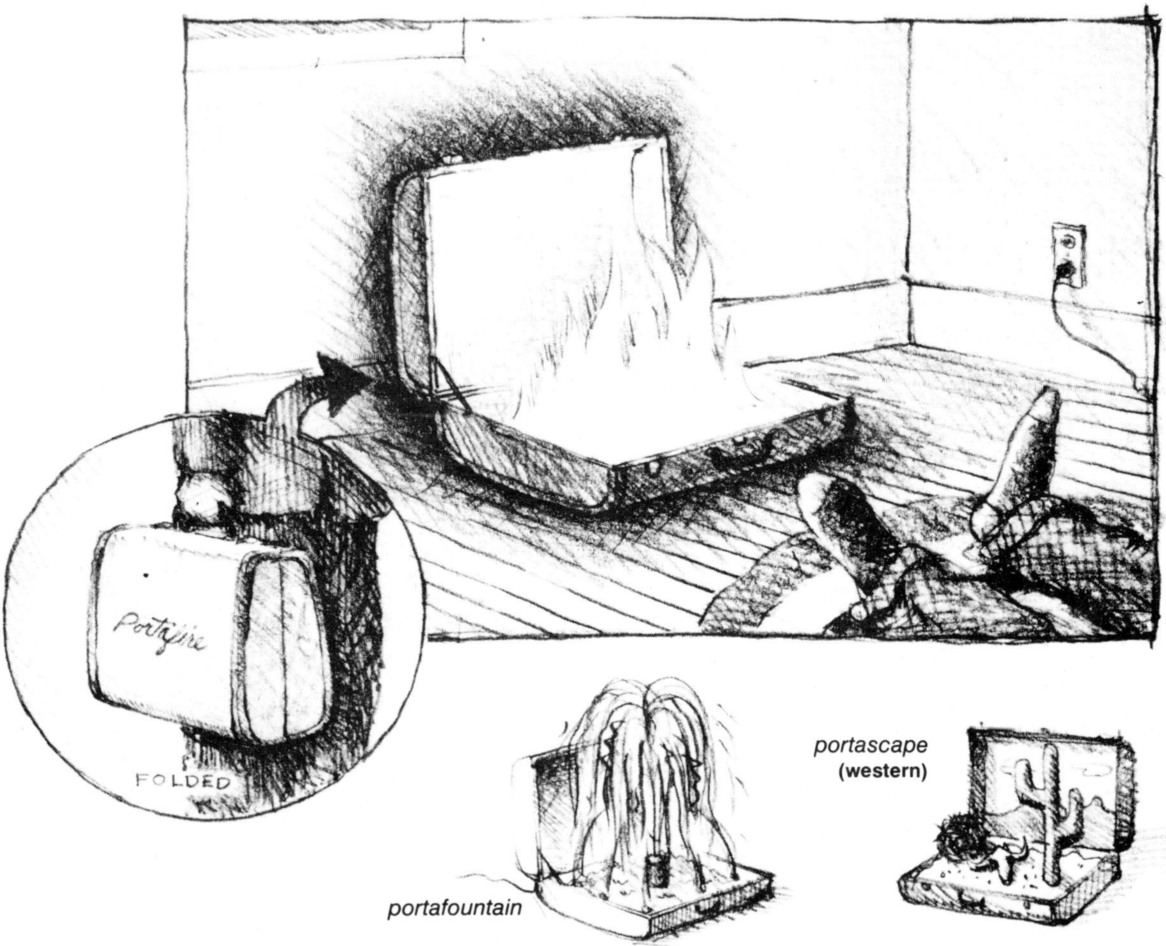

FLIPPED INN

HEART O' THE WORLD

global headquarters

replacement for United Nations

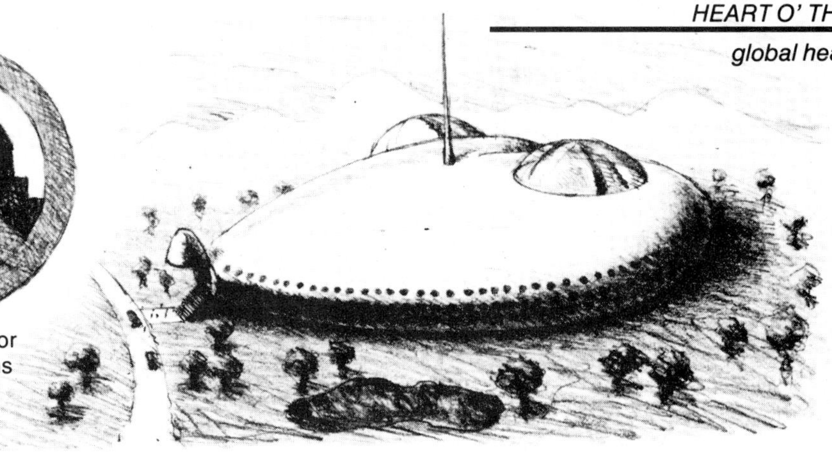

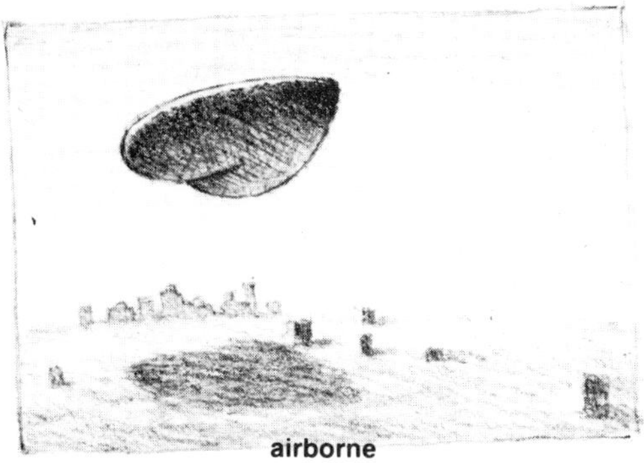

airborne

at sea

ROADSIDE "AUTOWATCH"

bleachers

TRANSIT BALL

"the invisible bridge"

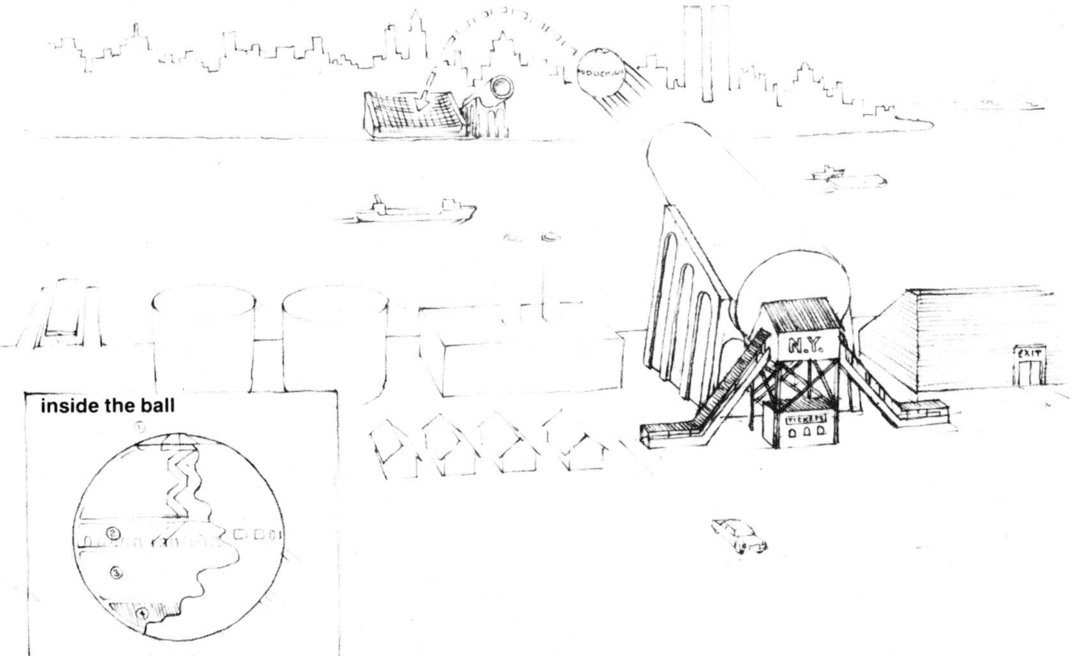

inside the ball

1. **observation dome**
2. **passenger deck**
3. **cargo hold**
4. **ballast**

DO-IT-YOURSELF THINKING
BONUS ESSAY

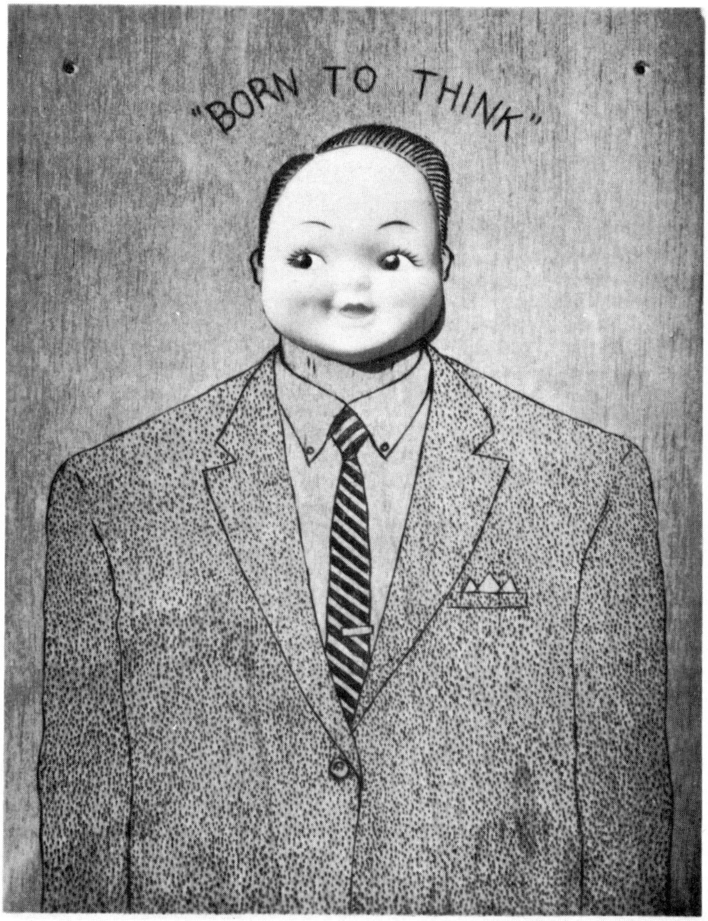

"BORN TO THINK"

The brain as man (artist's conception).

"HOW TO COME UP WITH AN IDEA"

(*NOTE:* It is erroneous to assume that an "idea" is always necessary to initiate the successful resolution of a piece of business. Be sure your problem cannot be solved by a more tangible expedient, such as "elbow grease.") The following suggestions are numbered for reference ease.

1. PICK A NICE PLACE TO THINK.

This, of course, will vary with the individual, so be advised to experiment freely.

(a) In bed, with the covers drawn up over your head and a stuffed animal (to be carefully selected) clutched tightly to the front of the body.

(b) On the road, behind the wheel of a large, heavy, quiet automobile, a "think tank," as it were. (Suggested: Buick Electra 225, Mercury Grand Marquis, Dodge Royal Monaco)

(c) While experiencing simultaneous physical and mental disorientation through performing an unusual public act. For example: Walk into a supermarket naked, on skis, with a TV case over your head.

(d) Avoid at all costs sitting at a neat, well-lit table with clean paper and a half dozen sharpened pencils.

(e) Fresh air affectionados should heed this tip: attach an old light bulb to a stick and push into the ground near your location. This will warn others that you are "thinking" and not to disturb.

2. IF AN IDEA WON'T COME.

Don't panic. The thought process, like other bodily functions, may need an occasional "push" to get started.

(a) Confuse yourself. Sometimes order emerges out of a state of chaos. Attempt to think in tongues. Try to see out of your knees. Pretend that bowling trophies grow from seeds.

(b) Win the confidence and friendship of your brain by the simple expedient of giving it a name. If your name is Bob, try calling your brain "Little Bob."

3. TAKE CARE OF YOUR IDEA.
If you have not yet had an idea, stop. Re-read steps one and two.

(a) Carry a small notebook bound in leather, with the words, "My Ideas" embossed in gold on the cover. (Note: Forget the cheap scribble pad. Ideas symbolize the highest intellectual pursuits of man and deserve the very best.) Write down your ideas the minute they pop into your head.

(b) Never use a tape recorder to document your idea(s) unless you are certain no one else in the immediate vicinity is conversant in your language. Sad as it is, prodigious probing is plagued by plagiarism.

(c) A further word on security: reverting for a moment to our discussion of locations, I would like to recommend the Communist Bloc countries of eastern Europe. Not only is the language barrier almost insurmountable, but capitalist conceptualizing is of little interest to the local populace. And on a more subjective note, the famous scientist/inventor, Nikola Tesla, one of the most original thinkers of all time, was a native of eastern Europe. He was able to design a motor, subject it to the severest abuse until it eventually failed, make the necessary modifications and repairs and go on with the testing . . . all in his head!

4. USE YOUR IDEA.
This is strictly optional and may be felt by some to impose a stifling reality on the ephemeral nature of pure inspiration, for it is seldom possible to implement one's idea without calling on the offices of the "real world." On the other hand, some may find a challenge in this and may possess the skills, intuition and raw guts which will give them at least a shadow of a chance of success. I number myself with the former group and, for this reason, decline to discuss the subject further. Let us then go on to the next topic.

"HOW TO GET RID OF YOUR IDEA"

As ironic as it seems, keeping your brainchild may be more trouble than it's worth. The process of bringing an idea to a state of fruition is an occupation in itself (see: Use your idea.) and leaves scant opportunity for the continued pursuit of creative innovation. It may be better to begin again with a clean slate, as in playing a game, and enjoy as often as possible that delicious moment at which the "light bulb goes off," so to speak, without the hindrance of "research and development syndrome." Here are several ways to purge an original concept.

1. TRY NOT TO THINK ABOUT IT.
(I first heard this phrase in a science fiction film. A reporter said it to a little girl whose parents had just been abducted by a monster from space.) This technique may be recommended on the basis of its simplicity, for it requires no hardware and/or interaction with other people. However, it presupposes a degree of mental discipline unusual in today's push-button world.

2. PASS IT OFF ON SOMEONE ELSE.
This is a very "down to earth" method of idea disposal which might be visualized as a game of "intellectual tag." Try telling your idea to a suspected plagiarist or, if unavailable, to any friend, relative, acquaintance or passerby who expresses a sufficient level of interest to effect the transfer. If a slight "creative residue" persists, select from the following expedients to complete the erasure: run an ad stating your idea in a local paper under "personals," place Xeroxed notes under hundreds of windshield wipers, and/or using the medium of environmental graffiti, spraycan your concept on the sides of buildings and mass-transit vehicles.

3. USE "THOUGHT REMOVER."
I prefer the cream type as opposed to the roll-on, as it penetrates more deeply when gently massaged into the temples. "Mental Floss" is said to be effective as well, but I have had no personal experience, at least to my recollection.

And with that I have expressed the sum total of my knowledge on the subject of "ideas." To those who asked the question that prompted this piece of extravagance, I hope no further comment is required as I have nothing to add. But to those who weren't interested in the first place and read this through a sheer excess of time, "bear" in mind that the brain is a funny "animal." One of these days, the legendary light bulb may go off over your head and you will thank me for the preceding words.

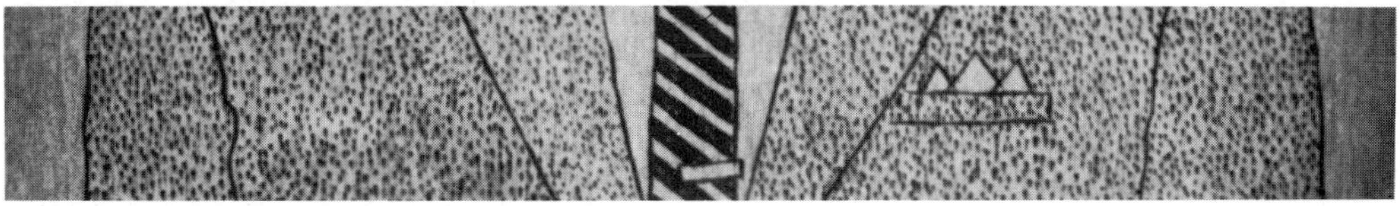

ABOUT THE AUTHOR

Philip Garner is an artist and inventor who sees himself as "an inventor in the spirit of Rube Goldberg." His previous book, the BETTER LIVING CATALOG (Delilah), featuring "62 Absolute Necessities For Contemporary Survival," continues to receive international acclaim for its comic inspiration and social satire. Garner also contributed the introduction and commentary for RUBE GOLDBERG: A RETROSPECTIVE (Delilah). His work has appeared in museums and galleries across America and Europe, and in magazines such as Playboy, Reader's Digest, Esquire and Rolling Stone. Raised in Naperville, Illinois, Philip Garner lives and works in Hollywood.